CUBA
the culture

April Fast and Susan Hughes
Consulting Author Dr. Keith Ellis

Principal photography by Marc Crabtree

A Bobbie Kalman Book
The Lands, Peoples, and Cultures Series

Crabtree Publishing Company
www.crabtreebooks.com

The Lands, Peoples, and Cultures Series

Created by Bobbie Kalman

Coordinating editor
Ellen Rodger

Project editor
Carrie Gleason

Production coordinator
Rosie Gowsell

Project development, design, editing, and photo research
First Folio Resource Group, Inc.
Erinn Banting
Quinn Banting
Molly Bennett
Tom Dart
Claire Milne
Jaimie Nathan
Debbie Smith
Meighan Sutherland
Anikó Szocs

Prepress and printing
Worzalla Publishing Company

Consulting Author
Dr. Keith Ellis, Professor Emeritus, University of Toronto, Doctor Honoris Causa, University of Havana

Consultants
Grenville Draper, Florida International University, Department of Geology; John Kirk, Department of Spanish, Dalhousie University

Photographs
AFP/Corbis/magmaphoto.com: p. 7 (left), p. 11 (bottom); Art Archive/Mireille Vautier: p. 21 (top); Sophie Bassouls/Corbis Sygma/magmaphoto.com: p. 28 (right); Jeremy Bembaron/ Corbis/magmaphoto.com: p. 16 (top); David Bergman/ Corbis/magmaphoto.com: p. 19 (right); Richard Bickel/ Corbis/magmaphoto.com: p. 7 (right); Tibor Bognar/ Corbis/magmaphoto.com: p. 27 (bottom); Jan Butchofsky-Houser/Corbis/magmaphoto.com: p. 17 (top); Marc Crabtree: title page, p. 4, p. 5 (bottom), p. 10, p. 14 (both), p. 22, p. 24, p. 26, p. 28 (left), p. 29 (bottom); Claudia Daut/Corbis/ magmaphoto.com: p. 5 (top); James Davis Travel Photography: p. 15, p. 20 (left); Digital Image © The Museum of Modern Art/Licensed by SCALA/Art Resource, NY: p. 21 (bottom); Jonas Grau/Eye Ubiquitous: cover; Hulton Archive/Getty Images: p. 18 (bottom); Bob Krist/Corbis/magmaphoto.com: p. 11 (top), p. 18 (top); Jacques Langevin /Corbis Sygma/ magmaphoto.com: p. 9 (top); Julie Lemberger/Corbis/ magmaphoto.com: p. 16 (bottom); Christopher J. Morris/ Corbis/magmaphoto.com: p. 27 (top); Françoise de Mulder/ Corbis/magmaphoto.com: p. 8 (left); Amos Nachoum/ Corbis/magmaphoto.com: p. 3; Reuters NewMedia/ Corbis/magmaphoto.com: p. 6, p. 12 (bottom), p. 19 (left); Paul Seheult/Corbis/magmaphoto.com: p. 12 (top); Paul Seheult/ Eye Ubiquitous/Corbis/magmaphoto.com: p. 25 (left); Ronald Siemoneit/Corbis Sygma/magmaphoto.com: p. 29 (top); Smithsonian American Art Museum, Washington, DC/Art Resource, NY: p. 23; Snark/Art Resource: p. 20 (right); Trip/ Karen Mclaren: p. 25 (right); Trip/M. O'Brien: p. 17 (bottom); Robert Van der Hilst/Corbis/magmaphoto.com: p. 8 (right), p. 13 (top); David H. Wells/Corbis/magmaphoto.com: p. 9 (bottom); Nik Wheeler/Corbis/magmaphoto.com: p. 13 (bottom)

Illustrations
Sylvie Bourbonnière: pp. 30–31
Dianne Eastman: icon
David Wysotski, Allure Illustrations: back cover

Cover: A musician carries his double bass along the cobbled streets of Havana, Cuba's capital city.

Title page: A trumpeter plays during a street festival in the central city of Santa Clara.

Icon: *Tres* guitars, which appear at the head of each section, are played in many types of Cuban music. This type of guitar is called a *tres*, the Spanish word for three, because it has three pairs of strings.

Back cover: *Almiquí*, or Cuban solenodons, hide during the day in hollow trees or underground burrows, and come out at night to search for insects and spiders to eat.

Published by
Crabtree Publishing Company

PMB 16A,	612 Welland Avenue	73 Lime Walk
350 Fifth Avenue	St. Catharines	Headington
Suite 3308	Ontario, Canada	Oxford OX3 7AD
New York	L2M 5V6	United Kingdom
N.Y. 10118		

Cataloging-in-Publication Data

Hughes, Susan, 1960-
  Cuba. The culture / Susan Hughes & April Fast.
    p. cm. -- (Lands, peoples & cultures)
  Includes index.
  ISBN 0-7787-9326-5 (RLB) -- ISBN 0-7787-9694-9 (pb)
  1. Cuba--Civilization--Juvenile literature. I. Fast, April, 1968- II. Title. III. Lands, peoples, and cultures series.
  F1760.H84 2004
  972.91--dc22
                              2004000806
                                 LC

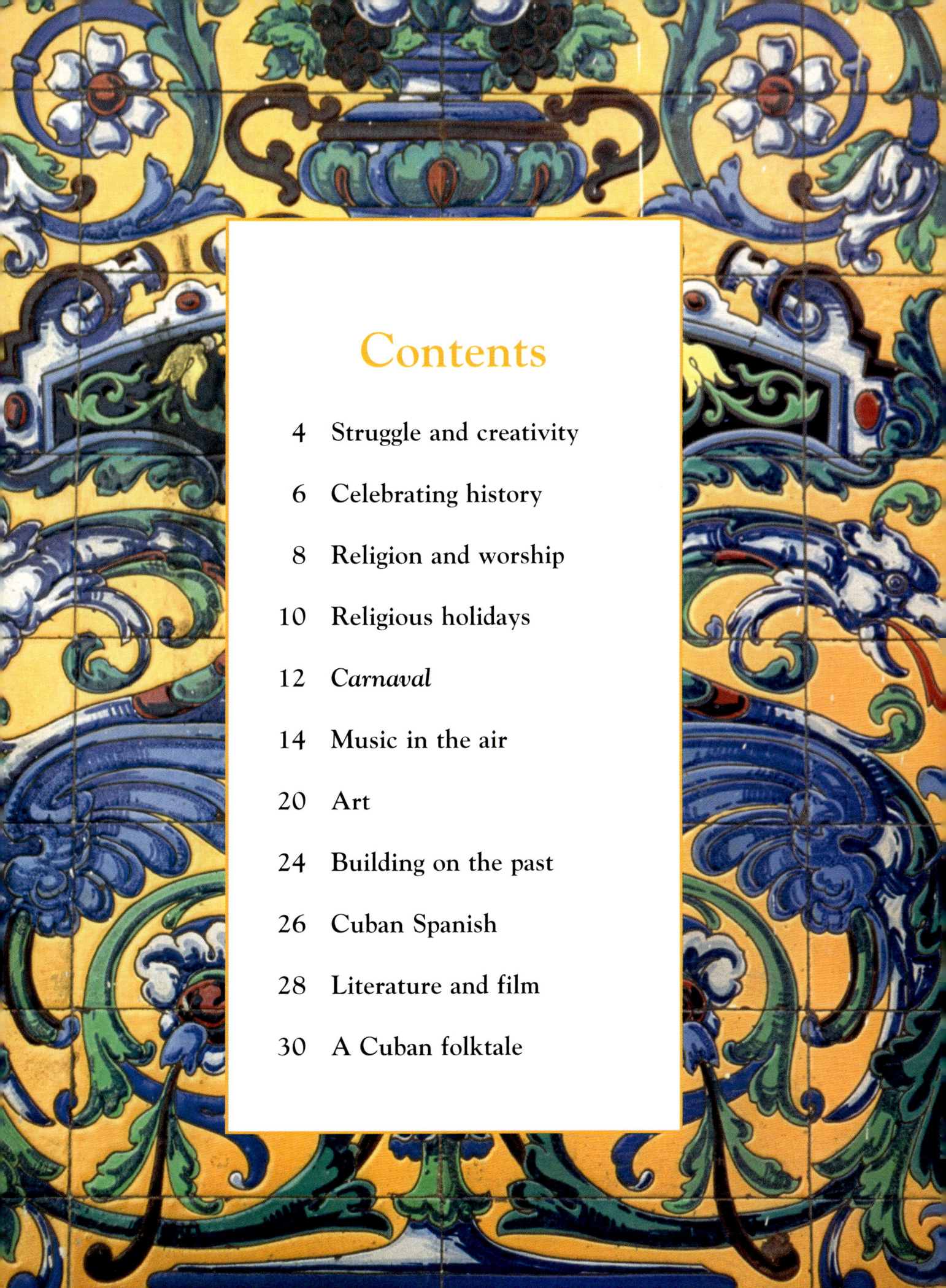

Contents

4   Struggle and creativity

6   Celebrating history

8   Religion and worship

10   Religious holidays

12   *Carnaval*

14   Music in the air

20   Art

24   Building on the past

26   Cuban Spanish

28   Literature and film

30   A Cuban folktale

 # Struggle and creativity

Musicians in Havana, Cuba's capital city, play traditional music on guitars and shakers called maracas.

The people who live on the island of Cuba, in the Caribbean Sea, are deeply involved in the politics of their country. In 1959, a young lawyer named Fidel Castro became Cuba's leader. He introduced **Communism**, a system in which the government owns and controls a country's businesses, **natural resources**, and industries, and helps its people by funding education, cultural, health care, and housing programs.

Struggle and support

Many Cubans were unhappy with Castro's new government, and some spoke out against Communism. Some of those who did were **censored** or jailed. Some artists, musicians, writers, and religious leaders felt they were no longer allowed to express themselves freely through their work. Many left to live in countries such as the United States and England.

Other artists supported Castro's reforms and stayed in Cuba. Castro's government began **investing** money in the arts, which made it possible for more artists to develop their talents. Galleries, exhibitions, and festivals that showcase Cuban art, music, and literature are funded and strictly controlled by the Cuban government.

Common themes

No matter where they live or what their political views are, Cuban artists and writers show their love for their island and ties to their **ancestors** in their work. Their ancestors include the Taíno, who came to Cuba from South America around 1200 B.C.; the Spanish, who **colonized** the island for more than 400 years beginning in the 1500s; and the tens of thousands of West Africans who were brought to Cuba to work as slaves on sugar cane, tobacco, and coffee **plantations**.

Schoolchildren toss flowers into the sea on October 28 to remember Cuban hero Camilo Cienfuegos. Cienfuegos helped Castro establish a new government. Shortly afterward, his plane was lost at sea.

Children wear costumes for a street festival in Sancti Spíritus, a city in central Cuba. People sing, dance, and play musical instruments during the festival.

Celebrating history

Many of Cuba's festivals honor the country's fight for independence. October 10 is *Grito de Yara*, or "the Shout of Yara." This holiday remembers the start of the Ten Years' War, in 1868. The war began when Carlos Manuel de Céspedes and 37 other wealthy landowners freed their slaves, attacked the southwestern town of Yara, and declared Cuba's independence from Spain. People celebrate *Grito de Yara* by attending lectures about Cuba's heroes and by watching reenactments of historical battles.

February 24 is *Grito de Baire*, or "the Shout of Baire." During this holiday, Cubans remember the final stages of the war in which they fought for independence from Spain, from 1895 to 1898. The war began when General Saturnino Lora, a leader of the Cuban Revolutionary Party, rallied troops in the southeastern town of Baire to fight against the Spanish.

The National Rebellion

The Celebration of the National Rebellion begins on July 26 and lasts three days. It honors the day in 1953 when Fidel Castro led a group of **rebels** in an attack against the **dictatorship** of General Fulgencio Batista. Batista's government was not providing good housing, medical care, and education for the Cuban people. Castro failed to overthrow Batista's government in the attack, but the rebellion was still considered a success because it encouraged thousands of Cubans to join the **revolutionary** movement.

As part of the festival, popping firecrackers and colorful lanterns light up the streets. Art exhibits and music and dance performances depict the rebellion, and thousands of people listen to Castro speak about Cuba's past and future.

Cuban president Fidel Castro joins a crowd in the western city of Pinar del Río for the Celebration of the National Rebellion. People wave the Cuban flag during parades and speeches to show their support of their country.

New Year's Day and Liberation Day

Cubans mark two important events on January 1 — New Year's Day and Liberation Day, the day Fidel Castro took control of Cuba in 1959. On New Year's Eve, people feast on *lechón asado*, a whole pig soaked in a sweet, spicy sauce, wrapped in banana leaves, and roasted over a fire pit for five hours. On New Year's Day, Cubans wake early to hear a **patriotic** speech by Castro, which is broadcast on radio and television. The rest of the day is spent relaxing and visiting with friends. Some people celebrate the new year by tossing buckets of water off their balconies. This symbolizes throwing away their problems.

A farmer from the southern city of Cienfuegos weighs a turkey that he is selling for a New Year's Eve meal. Cubans celebrate New Year's Eve with friends and family by preparing a large feast.

(above) Parades on May 19 remember Cuban hero José Martí, who died on this day in 1895 fighting to free Cuba from Spanish rule.

La Fiesta del Fuego

La Fiesta del Fuego, or "the Festival of Fire," is held each July in the southeastern city of Santiago de Cuba. The festival celebrates the accomplishments of artists, musicians, writers, and dancers from Cuba and other Caribbean islands. Each year, a different Cuban hero is honored at the week-long event. People attend lectures, parades, and performances that celebrate the hero, and they go to art galleries, readings of stories and poetry, and theaters to see concerts, dance performances, and films by people from Cuba and the Caribbean.

Drummers perform at a Santería ceremony. Drums are an important part of the ceremonies because people believe the drums help them communicate with spirits called orishas.

Cubans have experienced periods when religion was encouraged and other periods when it was forbidden. For example, in the past, the Taíno believed in gods and goddesses that controlled nature. They carved figures called *zemis* that represented these spirits, and kept them in their homes for luck and protection. When the Spanish settled in Cuba in 1511, they forced the Taíno to **convert** to Roman Catholicism. Roman Catholicism is a **denomination** of Christianity. Christians believe in one God and in the teachings of his son, Jesus Christ.

Santería

Slaves brought to work on Cuba's plantations introduced their own religious traditions to Cuba. Many slaves were Yoruban, a people from present-day Nigeria, in West Africa. They worshiped Olorun, the highest god in the Yoruban religion, and hundreds of *orishas*, or spirits, who they believed protected people and brought them good health, money, and love.

Like the Taíno, West Africans were forced to convert to Roman Catholicism by Spanish plantation owners. They developed a religion, Santería, that helped them keep their beliefs alive. Santería combined Yoruban and Roman Catholic beliefs by matching *orishas* with Roman Catholic **saints**. For example, Babaluayé, the *orisha* of sickness and health, is associated with Saint Lazarus, the Catholic saint of people with a disease called leprosy. The Spanish thought the Yoruba were worshiping the saints, but they were really worshiping their own spirits.

Practicing Santería

Santería is the most popular religion in Cuba today. As in the past, ceremonies take place in the homes of religious leaders called *santeros* and *santeras*. Worshipers often **sacrifice** chickens or goats as gifts to the *orishas*, or leave food and small gifts at **shrines**. In addition, each *orisha* has a festival day, which is celebrated with dances, songs, and the beating of drums.

Santería followers leave offerings of food, herbs, and flowers at shrines in the homes of santeros and santeras. Statues of Catholic saints and stones representing the orishas also rest on the shrine.

Religion and the revolution

Before Castro's rule, Roman Catholicism was Cuba's official religion. The Roman Catholic Church held a great deal of power, including controlling the education system. After the revolution, Castro wanted the government, not a religion, to be the most powerful institution and he did not recognize any official religion. People were allowed to worship any religion they chose, but public ceremonies and religious holidays were banned. Until the 1990s, anyone who worshiped openly was also not allowed to join the Communist political party, which meant they could have no say in the country's government and government policy.

Religion today

In 1992, changes to Cuba's **constitution** guaranteed complete religious freedom to all Cubans. Today, nearly 65 percent of the population practices Santería. Another 23 percent are Roman Catholic. People also follow other African religions, such as Abakuá and Congo, and other denominations of Christianity, such as the Baptist Church, Lutheranism, and Anglicanism. American missionaries introduced these denominations of Christianity to Cuba in the early 1900s, when the U.S. controlled the island.

Roman Catholics celebrate mass in a Havana cathedral. Cuba has no official religion.

A rabbi, or Jewish religious leader, recites a prayer in a Havana synagogue. The government has provided funding to restore historic synagogues and other buildings in Habana Vieja, or Old Havana.

 # Religious holidays

Before 1998, religious holidays, such as Christmas and Easter, were normal work days. Christmas celebrates the birth of Jesus Christ, and Easter celebrates his death and resurrection, or return to life. Today, more Cuban Christians are celebrating these holidays.

Christmas

Cubans decorate their homes with Christmas trees, tinsel, paper chains, and wreaths a few days before Christmas. On December 24, Christmas Eve, they attend a midnight church service called *Noche Buena*, or "Good Night." In the past, people called this service *Misa del gallo*, or "Mass of the Rooster," because it lasted almost until dawn, when the rooster crowed to mark a new day. Today, the services are shorter.

After church, people gather with family and friends for a feast of pork, rice, beans, and a root vegetable called yuca. They drink, dance, and sing until early morning. On Christmas Day, December 25, Cubans go to churches to see the *nacimientos*, or nativity scenes. These scenes, made up of sculptures, tell the story of Jesus Christ's birth.

Las Parrandas de Remedios

On Christmas Eve, the town of Remedios, in northern Cuba, hosts a noisy parade called *Las Parrandas de Remedios*, or the Remedios *Fiesta*. Some people believe that this tradition started hundreds of years ago, when a priest sent boys with clanging bells and shaking rattles to wake people up for the midnight church service on Christmas Eve.

Today, for *Las Parrandas de Remedios*, the town divides itself into two groups, the Carmelitas, from the El Carmen neighborhood, and the Sansaríes, from the San Salvador neighborhood. The groups prepare elaborate floats for a parade, dress in fancy costumes, and play music on instruments such as cowbells, drums, and trumpets. Then, they hold a competition to see who has the best costumes and floats. After the parade, spectators enjoy a fireworks display.

The residents of Santa Clara celebrate their city with a large street festival. For many years, religion was not part of many Cubans' lives, so cities began festivals that celebrated other aspects of Cuban culture.

Exchanging gifts

Cubans exchange gifts on January 6, *El Día de los Reyes Magos*, or the Feast of Kings. The holiday celebrates the three kings who Christians believe followed a star to find the baby Jesus in the town of Bethlehem, where he was born. Children believe that if they are good, the kings will bring them gifts like the ones they brought for the baby Jesus. On the night before *El Día de los Reyes Magos*, children place grass in shoeboxes to feed the kings' camels. When the children wake up, the grass is gone and their shoeboxes are filled with gifts.

The *Fiesta* in El Cobre

La Fiesta de la Virgen de la Caridad del Cobre, or the Festival of the Virgin of Mercy of El Cobre, celebrates Cuba's **patron saint**, the Virgin Mary. The Virgin Mary was Jesus Christ's mother. According to legend, three Cuban fishers caught in a storm found a statue of the Virgin Mary floating in the choppy waters. Miraculously, they safely reached the shore and believed that the statue guided them there. The fishers then placed the statue on display in a church in the southeastern town of El Cobre. Today, people celebrate *La Fiesta de la Virgen de la Caridad del Cobre* on September 8 by visiting the church where the statue is displayed.

People travel from all over Cuba to see the famous statue of the Virgin Mary in the Basílica del Cobre.

Christians in Cuba celebrate Easter in March or April by attending church services and holding Easter parades, in which they carry pictures of Jesus and large crosses, a symbol of Christianity, through the streets.

 # Carnaval

Carnaval is a lively festival that blends African and Catholic customs. Traditionally, *Carnaval* took place before Lent, the 40 days before Easter. During Lent, Christians give up certain foods and drinks to remember the suffering of Jesus Christ. *Carnaval* developed as a way for them to have fun, feast, dance, and sing before the solemn period of Lent began.

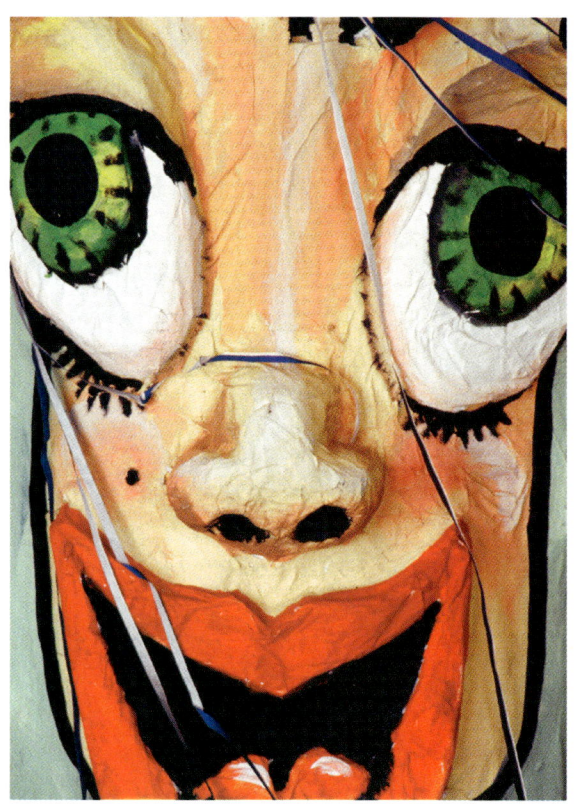

(right) Some Carnaval parades feature giant masks made from papier-mâché. To make papier-mâché, strips of paper soaked in glue are layered onto a wire frame. When dry, the masks are painted to resemble people, animals, and other creatures.

(below) Girls adjust their Carnaval costumes before joining a parade through the city of Santiago de Cuba. People spend weeks before the celebrations making their elaborate costumes.

(above) Musicians playing drums weave through the streets of Santiago de Cuba during Carnaval.

A changing festival

When Castro came to power, he did not want Cubans to celebrate *Carnaval* in the midst of *zafra*, the sugar cane harvest. He moved the festival from before Lent to the third weekend in July, just before the Celebration of the National Rebellion. Today, most cities still celebrate *Carnaval* in July, although Havana celebrates the festival in the spring.

Cuba's largest *Carnaval* celebration takes place in Santiago de Cuba. Each neighborhood organizes a dance group, called a *comparsa*, that joins a parade through the city's streets. The dancers wear colorful costumes and are accompanied by singers, drummers, and other musicians walking or riding on decorated floats. People wave *estandartes*, or banners that show the name of their neighborhood.

Thousands of Cubans in the United States continue to celebrate Cuban festivals. The city of Miami, in Florida, has a two-week celebration of Cuban culture, ending with a colorful Carnaval parade.

Music in the air

In Cuba's rainforests and along its beaches lie materials that Cubans have used to make musical instruments. The Taíno made instruments out of wood and **conch shells**. They filled **gourds** with dried beans, seeds, and pebbles to make maracas, and scratched notches into gourds to make *güiros*, which they played by running sticks along them.

Instruments from West Africa

West Africans brought to Cuba various types of drums. The long, narrow *batá* drums are covered with animal skins at both ends. Musicians hold the drums across their laps or place them on stands so they can play either end. They make the sound higher or lower by hitting different parts of the drum's surface. *Batá* drums are called "talking drums" because the changes in **pitch** are similar to the way people's voices change when they speak.

Conga drums, which were first made in Cuba, are waist high, and musicians play them standing up. To produce higher and lower sounds, drummers tap different parts of the drumskin.

Made in Cuba

Over time, Cubans began to invent their own instruments. Many of the instruments were made by farmers in an eastern region called Oriente, where **immigrants** with different musical traditions settled. The *tres* is a small guitar with three pairs of strings. Bongo drums are two drums connected by a wooden bar. Musicians hold the drums in their laps. *Guayos* are similar to *güiros*, but they are made of metal. The *marímbula* is a hollow wooden box with metal strips that are plucked with the fingers. *Claves* are two wooden sticks that are tapped together to create the main rhythm of Cuban music.

Musicians playing tres, maracas, and guitars perform outdoors in Havana.

In this son *group, the vocalist, guitar players,* tres *player, and upright bass player provide the melody, while percussionists tap out the beat on bongo drums and* claves.

Son

The songs and dances that Cuban musicians, singers, and dancers perform blend instruments and styles from different times in history and different countries. The *son* is Cuba's national music and dance, and is the basis of many types of music in **Latin America**. *Son* began as a style of folk music sung on coffee and sugar cane plantations in Oriente during the late 1800s. Musicians playing *tres* and bongos sang poetic songs about love, humor, and patriotism.

As *son*'s popularity spread throughout Cuba, especially to Havana in the 1920s, guitars, *claves*, and maracas became part of the sound. Over time, people added faster rhythms and different instruments to change the style. *Son* bands now use accordions, synthesizers, violins, trumpets, and trombones, and the lyrics of modern *son* music tell about life in Cuba today.

Buena Vista Social Club

In the late 1940s, a large group of *son* musicians played in a band at the popular Buena Vista Social Club, in Havana. When Fidel Castro came to power, some of the musicians moved to other parts of Cuba or they left the island, and the group **disbanded**. Some of those who stayed took jobs as laborers to earn a living.

In 1999, some musicians who played at the famous club were reunited to produce a CD called *Buena Vista Social Club*. Some of these musicians were almost 90 years old. A documentary movie also followed band members as they told stories about playing in Cuba and the U.S. during the 1940s.

Trova music

Hundreds of years ago, Spanish singers called *trovadores* traveled from town to town in Cuba playing guitars and singing folk songs called *trovas*. In the 1960s, singers Silvio Rodríguez (1946–) and Pablo Milanés (1943–) created a new style of *trova* called *la nueva trova*, or "the new *trova*." *La nueva trova* uses synthesizers and electric guitars, and its lyrics tell about love, daily life, and social and political issues in Cuba and around the world. Today, every major city has a *casa de trova*, or "house of *trova*," where audiences listen to singers and musicians perform.

Bolero

The slow, romantic *trova* developed into a style of song called the *bolero*. At first, the *bolero* was played only on guitars, and then bongos, conga drums, maracas, and *claves* were added to the music. The popularity of the *bolero* spread to other Caribbean islands and to Spain, where the music was slowed down. One of Cuba's best-known *bolero* singers is Ibrahim Ferrer (1927–). In 1999, he won a Latin Grammy Award for his album *Buena Vista Social Club Presents ... Ibrahim Ferrer.*

Bolero singer Ibrahim Ferrer became famous outside of Cuba when he was 70 years old, after the release of the film Buena Vista Social Club.

Two dancers from the Ballet Nacional de Cuba perform. Alicia Alonso (1922–) founded Cuba's national ballet school and dance company with help from the government. Before founding the company, Alonso recovered from a serious car accident to become a famous ballerina.

In some Cuban dances, women wear ruffled skirts that they twirl and swing in time to the music.

Time to _rumba!_

One of the most popular forms of folk music in Cuba is the _rumba_. The _rumba_ began as a lively song with syncopated, or irregular, rhythms. Today, there are several styles of _rumba_, all of which involve a lead singer and chorus singing back and forth to one another.

Each style of _rumba_ has its own dance. The _guaguancó_ style is a slow dance performed by a man and a woman. The dance tells the story of a man trying to win over a woman's affections. In the lively _colombia_ style, male dancers try to impress one another by performing increasingly difficult dance steps. The _yambú_ style is very slow. The lyrics tell tales of long ago as the dancers imitate the slow, shaky steps of elderly people.

Many Cubans take classes to learn the complicated steps of rumbas and other dances. They practice what they learn at street parties called rumbones.

Country dance

The *zapateo* is a folk dance that was once popular throughout Cuba and is now performed mostly in the countryside. The name *zapateo* comes from the Spanish word *zapato*, or "shoe," which refers to the hard-soled shoes that dancers wear as they stamp their feet in time to the music. The dance was inspired by Spanish *flamenco* music, which is played on a guitar.

Mambo

Mambo is a style of music and dance that became popular in the 1930s and 1940s. Cuban composer Orestes López (1908–) combined a type of classical music from Europe, called the *danzón*, with faster African-style drum beats in a song called *"Mambo."* Inspired by López, musician Dámaso Pérez Prado (1916–1989) began writing songs in the *mambo* style, with quick notes played on drums and brass instruments. The music gained popularity in North America in the early 1950s when Prado and his band toured the United States. A style of dance in which couples sway their hips as they move back and forth developed from the catchy music.

Cultural organizations sponsor performances and workshops to teach people traditional Cuban folk dances.

Dámaso Pérez Prado became known as "King of the Mambo" as he toured throughout North America with his orchestra.

The *chachachá*

The music and dance called the *chachachá*, which also has its roots in the *danzón*, was first played in Havana in 1953 by orchestras called *charangas*. Singers sang the *chachachá*'s verses, while flutes, violins, conga drums, pianos, and bass guitars chimed in at the chorus. The *chachachá* gets its name from the sound of dancers' feet following the music's rhythm.

Salsa

Salsa, which means "sauce," combines the sounds of Cuban, African, American, and Caribbean music. This style of music, which developed in the late 1960s and early 1970s, is played by large bands that include a piano, bass, and horn section. The strong beat of the music comes from drums, *claves*, and *güiros*. As the music plays, *salsa* dancers twist their lower bodies and move their feet and arms in quick, complicated ways, all the while keeping their upper bodies straight.

Timba

Timba is a type of dance music based on *son*. The lead singers of *timba* groups shout, rap, and sing choruses over the background music. Audiences memorize the lyrics, which tell about love, life in Cuba, and Santería, and rap along with the performers. The most popular *timba* group is Cubanismo.

Modern music

Today, music in Cuba mixes many styles. *Son-bará* combines *son* with the beat of the *batá* drum, while *batá-rumba* combines the *rumba* with the *batá* drum beat. Mozambique is a mix of the *mambo* and the *conga* drum beat. Popular band Carlos Manuel y su Clan blends *timba*, *son*, and *salsa* music with jazz, reggae, hip hop, and dance music.

(above) Gloria Estefan (1958–) was born in Havana, but was raised in the United States. In 1975, she joined a group called the Miami Sound Machine. Since then, she has recorded ballads, disco, pop, and salsa music in English and Spanish.

(left) Celia Cruz (1924–2003) was a famous Cuban singer who was nicknamed "the Queen of Salsa." In 1950, she began singing on the radio with the popular orchestra Sonora Matancera. In the 1960s, Cruz left Cuba to start a career in the United States.

had a strong impact on art. The walls, stained glass windows, and carvings in the large churches that the Spanish built were decorated with elaborate, realistic images of people from the Bible.

A new Cuban style

The realistic style introduced from Spain inspired Cuban artists to paint scenes from life on their island. Eduardo Laplante (1818–1860) was a **lithographer** who created detailed images of rural life in Cuba, particularly of sugar cane plantations. The painting *Paisaje*, or *Landscape*, by Esteban Chartrand (1840–1883) shows images of *bohíos*, which are rural homes made from royal palm trees, in rich shades of green, brown, red, and blue. In his most famous painting, *Los Guajiros*, or *The Peasants*, Eduardo Abela (1889–1965) shows a group of peasants dressed in white hats and jackets on their way to a rooster fight.

The Taíno first created paintings of birds, fish, lizards, and people on cave walls more than 3,000 years ago. Scientists study these paintings to learn more about early life on the island.

Along the southwestern coast of Cuba, paintings created by the Taíno long ago still decorate cave walls. The paintings show hundreds of black and red circles and crosses that some **historians** believe were once used as calendars. The Taíno also made jewelry and pottery shaped like humans and animals, and they sculpted stone, shell, and bone into *zemis*, which represented gods and goddesses.

European influence

When the Spanish arrived in the 1500s, European styles of art began to influence art in Cuba. Roman Catholicism, introduced by the Spanish,

Eduardo Abela's painting Los Guajiros *celebrates peasant life in Cuba's countryside.*

HAND MADE

FABRICA DE TABACOS

IMPORTED FROM CUBA

El Triunfador

This cigar label from the late 1800s shows tobacco plants growing in the Cuban countryside.

Cigar art

In the 1800s, Cuban cigars, rolled by hand from the island's tobacco crops, were shipped to countries such as the United States and Britain. The cigars were each wrapped in colorful paper and packed together in boxes. Cigar companies began to hire artists to create beautiful wrappers and boxes to advertise their brands. The artists created designs that showed Cubans in scenes from everyday life. These designs were carved into metal plates. The plates were coated with ink and stamped onto paper in a process called lithography. Many people collect the beautiful boxes and wrappers.

Cuban artist Mariano Rodríguez (1912–1990) became well known in the 1940s for his colorful paintings of roosters.

Artists carefully add color to a giant mural. The Cuban government hires artists to paint murals to help make Cuba's cities more beautiful.

Poster art

Poster art is a style of art that became popular after Castro's rise to power. Using a technique called **silk-screening**, artists created large, colorful posters that celebrated Communism, the revolution, and Cuba's national heroes. Poster artist Félix René Mederos (1933–1996) painted enormous posters, including a series of fourteen panels depicting Ernesto "Che" Guevara, a doctor from Argentina who helped the poor in several Latin American countries before joining Castro's revolutionary cause in 1956.

Papier-mâché

Brothers Filiberto and Yanoski Mora create art with papier-mâché. They layer pieces of paper soaked in glue over a Styrofoam base to create three-dimensional objects. The Mora brothers are best known for their life-sized papier-mâché vehicles, including a Harley Davidson motorcycle, complete with moving parts, and a bus full of passengers, including a priest with a rooster on his knee, a country music singer, tourists, a woman with a baby, and a soldier.

Modern art

Cuban artist Wilfredo Lam (1902–1982) began his career creating surreal, or dreamlike, paintings. His style changed after working with Pablo Picasso, a well-known Spanish artist. Picasso introduced Lam to cubism, a style of painting in which people and objects appear to be broken into small pieces and stuck together again. Lam combined cubism with African sculpture, legends, and religious images from Santería in his own style of art.

Rita Longa (1912–2000) created sculptures in metal and stone, including *La Bailarina*, or *The Ballerina*, which stands outside the Tropicana nightclub in Havana. Manuel Mendive (1944–) is an Afro-Cuban artist who paints and sculpts *orishas*. His painting *La Mariposa*, or *The Butterfly*, shows a bright yellow butterfly hovering above trees. The colors and details are so vibrant that the painting looks like a photograph.

Cuban artist Mario Carreño (1913–1999) incorporated elements of cubism and surrealism in paintings such as Cuba Libre.

Building on the past

Cuba's simple country homes, Spanish-style mansions, and modern concrete towers reflect the island's history. The earliest buildings in Cuba were built by the Taíno, who used the wood and leaves from royal palm trees to make their homes, called *bohíos*. *Bohíos* are still built in Cuba's countryside. People weave as many as a thousand royal palm leaves together to make the *bohío*'s waterproof roof.

Built to protect

When the Spanish settled in Cuba, they built towns and cities along the coasts. To protect their settlements from attack, they constructed stone fortresses. In 1589, Castillo de los Tres Santos Reyes Magos del Morro, or El Morro, was built to protect Havana's harbor. A deep dry moat, or ditch, surrounded the triangular fort. Inside were officers' quarters, stables, a chapel, dungeons, and a wine cellar. Across the harbor from El Morro, a smaller fort was constructed called Castillo de San Salvador de la Punta, or La Punta. If pirates or attackers were sighted, chains and logs were extended across the channel between the two forts to prevent intruders from entering the harbor.

Many tobacco farmers build small thatched bohíos *where they dry their tobacco leaves.*

Spanish colonial architecture

Many Spanish buildings still stand in Cuba. The Museo Romántico, in the southern city of Trinidad, was built in 1740. Today, the building houses a collection of antique furniture and dishware from Europe. The outside has tall pillars, window shutters, elaborate iron balconies, and other details similar to those on buildings in Spain. Spanish colonists also built many cathedrals, or large churches, in Cuba. The Havana Cathedral, completed in 1777, has two bell towers. At night, the outside is lit up so people can clearly see the carvings, pillars, and statues of saints that decorate the cathedral's walls.

(above) The Hotel Santiago de Cuba, built in 1991, soars over every other building in the southeastern city. This red, white, and blue steel tower is decorated with metal tubing.

Many buildings in Trinidad, such as the Museo Romántico, are protected by the United Nations Educational, Scientific, and Cultural Organization (UNESCO). UNESCO gives money to the government to restore old buildings in Cuba.

Castro and architecture

After Castro came to power, his government paid **architects** to design new office buildings, schools, and apartments. The architects were told that their designs had to be simple and similar to one another so that buildings could be constructed quickly and inexpensively. As a result, many modern buildings in Cuba have the same boxlike design.

In recent years, tourism has become Cuba's strongest industry. To encourage even more tourists to visit the island, the government now allows architects who design hotels, restaurants, and resorts to show more creativity in their work.

 # Cuban Spanish

Taíno words that describe plants, animals, and other objects have become part of the English and Spanish languages. *Hamaca*, which means "hammock," *barbacoa*, which means "barbecue," and *iguana*, meaning the lizard "iguana," were originally Taíno words.

Unfortunately, most of the Taíno language has been lost. When the Spanish arrived in the 1500s, they forced the Taíno to speak Spanish. Spanish is now Cuba's official language. English and Creole, a language that combines French, English, and Spanish, are occasionally spoken on the island.

Cuban Spanish

Cuban Spanish is pronounced differently than European Spanish. In much of Spain, "ll" is pronounced like the letter "y" in English. In Cuba, "ll" is pronounced like the letter "l" in English. As a result, Spanish words, such as *camello*, which means "camel," are pronounced differently in each place. Cuban Spanish also has its own words, such as *guagua*, which means "bus." Other words in Cuban Spanish were influenced by African languages, such as Yoruba. For example, *cúmbila* is an African word that means "friend" in Cuban Spanish.

(top) Many books in Cuba's shops teach the people about their island's history.

English	Spanish
Yes.	*Sí.*
Please.	*Por favor.*
Thank you.	*Gracias.*
Good morning.	*Buenos días.*
Goodbye.	*Adiós.*
Pleased to meet you.	*Mucho gusto.*
How are you?	*¿Cómo está usted?*
Very well, thank you.	*Muy bien, gracias.*

Creole

Creole was brought to Cuba by French landowners who immigrated from Haiti. Haiti is a country on the nearby island of Hispaniola that was once a French colony. Some people think that Creole developed as a way for the French landowners to communicate with their slaves, who spoke different languages. Many Creole words are similar to English words. For example, *cav* means "cave" and *pijon* means "pigeon."

A father walks his daughter to school. Cuban students study both Spanish and English.

Friends chat in Spanish while playing dominoes. Cubans speak Spanish more quickly than people do in Spain.

 # Literature and film

A woman relaxes with a book written by a Cuban author.

The Taíno had no written language. They passed down their legends about the creation of the sun, moon, and sea by word of mouth. When the Spanish and Africans came to Cuba, they brought stories and legends from their **homelands**, which they also passed down by word of mouth.

Over time, Cubans began to write about their own lives and experiences on the island. Cirilo Villaverde y de la Paz (1812–1894) wrote many novels, including *Cecilia Valdés*, the story of a Cuban slave who falls in love with the son of her Spanish owner. The book was very important to Cubans because it described the connections between slaves and their owners. The story of *Cecilia Valdés* has been retold in an **operetta**, a film, and a ballet.

Afro-Cuban literature

Many West African slaves began to tell their own stories about their experiences in Cuba. Juan Francisco Manzano (1797–1854) was a slave who taught himself to read and write. He wrote a novel in Spanish called *Autobiografía de un esclavo*, or *Autobiography of a Slave*. It was the first book to describe the terrible treatment of slaves.

Alejo Carpentier (1904–1980) was another Cuban author who wrote about the culture of Afro-Cubans in a novel called *¡Ecue-Yamba-O!* His novel describes the traditions, music, and dance of Afro-Cubans.

Exile literature

Authors who left Cuba when Fidel Castro came to power developed a new style of writing known as "exile literature." This style of literature got its name because the people who wrote it felt that they had been exiled, or forced to leave their country, because their work opposed Communism and Fidel Castro's government. Many exile authors write about the beauty of Cuba, its people, and their feelings as outsiders in their new homes. Guillermo Cabrera Infante (1929–), who left Cuba for London, England in 1965, wrote *The Lost City*, a story about a young Cuban man forced to flee Cuba during the revolution.

Author Alejo Carpentier was imprisoned in 1928 for criticizing the government, and wrote his famous novel ¡Ecue-Yamba-O! in jail. In 1959, after Castro took leadership of Cuba, Carpentier became a professor at the University of Havana.

Cuban-American literature

Some authors whose families left Cuba for the United States write about their experiences in America. Oscar Hijuelos (1951–) wrote a novel about two Cuban brothers who moved to New York City in the 1950s to become *mambo* musicians. Hijuelos won the Pulitzer Prize, an annual prize for the best American novel. *The Aguero Sisters: A Novel,* by Cristina García (1959–), explores what being Cuban means to two sisters, one who left Cuba and the other who stayed.

Poetry

Cuban revolutionary hero José Martí (1853–1895) wrote many poems and essays about Cuban independence that are still studied in schools today. His poem *Versos sencillos* was set to music as *Guantanamera* and is now one of Cuba's most patriotic songs. Nicolás Guillén (1902–1989), who is considered Cuba's national poet, described the lives of average Cubans in his work, including a collection of eight poems called *Motivos de son.*

Film

Tomás Gutiérrez Alea (1928–1996) is considered one of Cuba's greatest directors of all time. His films include *Stories of the Revolution*, which describes events leading to Castro's victory. Humberto Solás (1941–) is a Cuban director and filmwriter. His film *Miel para Oshún*, or *Honey for Oshún*, tells the story of Roberto, an exiled Cuban living in the United States who returns to Cuba to look for his mother.

(below) Cuba's libraries and bookstores are full of bboks but many are old, or deal with the same subjet matter — the revolution and its heroes.

(above) Tomás Gutiérrez Alea's last film, Guantanamera, was a comedy about three people traveling to a small Cuban village for a funeral.

A Cuban folktale

Africans brought a rich tradition of storytelling to Cuba. Many of their stories explained how the world and the creatures in it came to be. Cubans still tell these stories, such as the story of how the rabbit got its long ears.

The rabbit's wishes

When the world was very young, Papá Dios, the god who created the whole world, filled it with plants, animals, rivers, and sunshine.

When Papá Dios was done, Conejo the rabbit came to visit him. "I want to be bigger," Conejo complained. "I have made you just the right size," Papá Dios replied.

Conejo did not agree. He insisted that he was too small to be noticed by anyone. "I will think about making you larger," Papá Dios said. "But before I make my decision, you must bring me three things: a feather from Águila the eagle, an egg from Serpiente the snake, and a tooth from León the lion."

"How can I do that?" Conejo wondered to himself, as he hopped away. "Those animals are so big and I am so small!" Conejo thought for a long time, and finally he had an idea. He made a whistle from a pumpkin stem and set off to find Águila the eagle.

When he found the large bird, he blew the whistle. "Stop blowing that whistle or I'll eat you! commanded Águila, who was bothered by the noise.

Conejo hid the whistle. "It's not actually a whistle, although it sounds like one," he explained. It's a magic hair that Papá Dios put in my fur to bring me supper each day. It doesn't work properly, though," he lied. "Today, all it brought me was fish. I only eat roots and green sprouts."

Águila, who loved to eat fish, asked Conejo for the hair. "Papá Dios must have made that hair for me," he insisted. "If you give it to me, I won't eat you."

"Okay," said Conejo and, as he pretended to put the hair on Águila, he slyly removed one of his feathers.

Encouraged by his success, Conejo went to look for Serpiente the snake. When he found her, he blew the whistle again, but this time he claimed that the magic hair brought only mice and rats.

"Why, those are my favorite foods," Serpiente hissed. "Papá Dios must have meant to give me the magic hair." Conejo agreed and, as he pretended to plant the hair in Serpiente's scales, he grabbed one of her eggs.

With the feather and egg in hand, Conejo set off to find León the lion. Now he complained that the whistling hair only brought goats and cows, León's favorite foods. Like Águila and Serpiente, León wanted the magic hair. So, Conejo asked León to close his eyes. As he pretended to plant the hair under León's chin, Conejo grabbed a rock and hit one of León's teeth with it.

León roared. "Oops," said Conejo. "That must have been one of the goats." With a quick pull, he yanked out León's tooth and escaped.

Conejo went straight to Papá Dios. "Here are the three things you asked for," he said proudly. Papá Dios smiled. "See?" he said. "This proves it. You are clever enough to take these three prizes from animals much larger than you. You don't need to be bigger. And," he continued, "you are already a big complainer. If I make you any bigger, you'll complain even more."

"But you broke your promise," Conejo whined. "You said you would make me bigger." So, Papá Dios reached out, grabbed Conejo's ears, and stretched them until they were very long. "There," he said. "Now you are bigger!"

Conejo was about to complain again, but then he stopped and felt his long ears. "Who knows what Papá Dios might do if I complain again," he thought. So with that, he hopped away. In time, he learned to love his long ears after all.

Glossary

ancestor A person from whom one is descended

architect A person who designs buildings

censored To have one's message changed because the government does not agree with it

colonize To establish and control a settlement in a distant country

Communism An economic system where a country's natural resources, businesses, and industry are owned by all the people and controlled by the government

conch shell The shell of a large sea snail, often used as a horn or trumpet

constitution A set of rules, laws, or customs of a government

convert To change one's religion, faith, or beliefs

denomination An organized religious group within a faith

dictatorship A government ruled by someone with complete power

disband To split up

gourd The hard-shelled fruit of certain vines

historian A person who studies history

homeland A country that is identified with a particular people or ethnic group

immigrant A person who settles in another country

invest To put money into a business

Latin America The Spanish-, French-, and Portuguese-speaking countries south of the United States

lithographer A person who creates images on metal plates, places ink on the images, then transfers them to paper

natural resource A material found in nature, such as oil, coal, minerals, or timber

operetta A musical that is similar to an opera, but has dialogue and is less serious

patriotic Full of love for one's country

patron saint A saint who is believed to protect a person, profession, city, or country

pitch The highness or lowness of a sound

plantation A large farm on which crops, such as cotton and sugar, are grown

rebel A person who opposes a government or ruler

revolutionary Relating to an uprising or war against a government

sacrifice To kill in a religious ceremony as an offering to the gods

saint A person through whom God performs miracles, according to the Christian Church

shrine A small area or structure dedicated to a god or saint

silk-screening A method of printmaking in which a design is put on a screen of silk or fine mesh. Ink is forced through the screen onto a printing surface.

 # Index

architecture 24–25
art 4, 20–23
bolero 16
Buena Vista Social Club 15
Carnaval 12–13
Castro, Fidel 4, 6, 7, 9, 13, 25
chachachá 19
Christianity 8, 9, 10–13, 20, 25
Christmas 10–11
cigar art 21
Creole 26, 27

Cruz, Celia 19
dance 13, 15, 16–19
Estefan, Gloria 19
Ferrer, Ibrahim 16
festivals 5, 6, 7, 10, 11, 12–13
films 29
folktales 28, 30–31
forts 24
heroes 5, 6, 7, 22, 29
holidays 6, 7, 10–11
languages 26–27
literature 4, 26, 28–29
mambo 18, 19

Martí, José 7, 29
music 4, 8, 10, 13, 14–19
musical instruments 8, 10, 13, 14, 15, 16, 18, 19
paintings 20, 21, 22, 23
papier-mâché 12, 22
parades 6, 7, 10, 11, 12, 13
poetry 29
poster art 22
religion 8–11, 12, 14, 20
Roman Catholicism 8, 9, 20
rumba 17, 19

salsa 19
Santería 8, 9
son 15, 19
Spanish 4, 6, 8, 16, 18, 20, 24, 25, 26–27, 28
Taíno 4, 8, 14, 20, 24, 26, 28
trovas 16
West Africans 4, 8, 12, 14, 26, 28, 30
writers 28–29

1 2 3 4 5 6 7 8 9 0 Printed in the U.S.A. 3 2 1 0 9 8 7 6 5 4